The English Vocabulary Builder

Lingo Valley Inc

ISBN: 9798551371540

For feedback or suggestions, please contact us at lingovalley@gmail.com

"If...we fail to master words, and if we allow their selection to be determined strictly by unconscious habit, we may be denigrating our entire experience of life. If you describe a magnificent experience as being "pretty good," the rich texture of it will be smoothed and made flat by your limited use of vocabulary.

People with an impoverished vocabulary live an impoverished emotional life; people with rich vocabularies have a multi-hued palette of colors with which to paint their experience, not only for others, but for themselves as well."

Anthony Robbins, Awaken the Giant Within

Why this book?

Words matter. They have the capacity to capture a special moment, elevate people's opinion of you, or resonate with an audience from a beautiful turn of phrase. But, when used incorrectly, words—and specifically a limited vocabulary—cripple our ability to describe experiences and articulate our thoughts and values.

The aim of this book is to not only enrich your vocabulary and way of speaking but to bring other people's words to life.

The book is appropriate for first-language and non-native English speakers.

Your surface lexicon and deep lexicon

Have you ever noticed that you tend to use far fewer words than those stored in your memory? The fact is that most people don't access the full range of words available in their memories when speaking or writing on a regular basis. Instead, people tend to rely on a more familiar set of words and phrases that they use regularly, pulled from their personal lexicon.

Your personal lexicon encompasses the words you recognize and employ in speech and writing. Within it, there exists both a surface lexicon and a deep lexicon. The former houses the words that unconsciously filter into daily conversations and writing, totaling approximately 1,500 to 3,000 unique words for a native English speaker. When you respond, compose sentences, or engage in dialogue, your brain initially consults your surface lexicon for familiar words.

The deep lexicon, meanwhile, encompasses approximately 20,000 to 30,000 unique words for the average English speaker, which are understood but seldom used in regular speech and writing.

To compare the difference between the surface and deep lexicons, let's consider two examples. To describe a monotonous speech, your automatic reaction might be to label it as "boring" or "uninteresting". However, there exist more precise and evocative terms like "loquacious" and "lackluster". Alternatively, imagine describing a breathtaking sunset; your immediate response might be "beautiful" or "amazing", yet there are more vivid choices available, like "awe-inspiring", "radiant", or "captivating". Regrettably, these more apt descriptions often remain untapped within the boundaries of your default vocabulary.

This prompts the question of how to best tap into your deep lexicon. How do you elevate known words, causing them to ascend from the depths of your deep lexicon and flourish into daily conversations? How do you impress people with your command of the language, and do you need to read the dictionary each night before you go to sleep?

The answer lies in repetition. A word's frequency of use strengthens its presence in your surface lexicon. According to a Yale study, around 38 repetitions are required for a word to transition into the surface lexicon of a non-native speaker learning English[1]. Native English speakers, too, require regular exposure and touch points with a word before they automatically default to it as part of their surface lexicon. Articulate individuals expand their surface lexicon through repetition rather than digging into their deep lexicon. Thus, with consistent practice and exposure to diverse contexts, you too can improve your ability to access and use a broader variety of words in your communication.

How to use new vocab

True articulation lies in deploying apt words at appropriate moments. While there's a temptation to use advanced vocabulary in everyday conversation and writing, you need to always be cognizant of your audience and avoid sounding ostentatious. Not everyone—especially second-language speakers—might understand what you mean when you describe something as "polychromatic". To help overcome this problem, it sometimes helps to provide a cue for understanding by leaving a hint or two in your next sentence. For example, "I love anything polychromatic. The compression of multiple colors always leaves me feeling mesmerized and curious."

In this example, the second sentence gently tells the reader the meaning of "polychromatic" without underestimating their

---

[1] Brendan Woo, "Effects of Short-Term Environment Change on Language Attrition: Cross-Linguistic Case Studies", *University of Yale*, 2008.

understanding. Also, adding context to your words doesn't need to be strictly limited to language. When you point to a polychromatic sports car, you don't need to elaborate, as the other person can deduce the meaning of polychromatic using visual clues.

How to use this book

To absorb and internalize the vocabulary contained in this book, it helps to focus on understanding the meaning of the word rather than trying to memorize set sentences. This approach gives you more bandwidth to remember individual words (rather than sentences) and helps you to use new vocab in a broader spectrum of use cases.

Finally, it's important to apply words in the correct context and understand the different feelings and emotions that words evoke. A *happy medium*, for example, conjures a different feeling than the word *sacrifice*, even though the two words can be used interchangeably in some situations.

Table of Contents

Ambidextrous

Type: Adjective

Ambidextrous is the quality of being able to use both hands with equal ease. Ambidextrous is the adjective form of the noun ambidexterity, which both originate from the Latin root words "ambi-" (meaning "both") and dexter (meaning "right"). As most people tend to be right-handed— it's said that only one in ten people use their left hand as much as their right hand for everyday tasks—the word dextrous generally applies to someone who favors their right hand.

While it usually refers to task-switching abilities such as writing with either hand, ambidextrous can also apply to other skills such as throwing a ball with either hand. In more rare cases, the term may extend to describing two separate forms of the same skill, such as short-form and long-form writing.

Sample Sentences

The pitcher is **ambidextrous**, he can pitch with his right or left arm.

Throughout history, there have been few cases of professional runners who were truly **ambidextrous** over short and long distances.

Quotes

I'm ambidextrous when I eat. But playing tennis right-handed - I can't do it. I'm clueless. *Rafael Nadal*

I've always been ambidextrous, writing short stories and novels, and I pretty much have been writing a novel and a handful of short stories every year since '91. *Catherine Ryan Hyde*

Question

Have you ever seen someone who was ambidextrous? For example, eating with a fork and knife or playing racquet sports using both hands interchangeably with ease.

Ambivalent

Type: Adjective

Ambivalent refers to having mixed or conflicting feelings about something or someone. It implies having both positive and negative emotions or thoughts simultaneously, leading to uncertainty or hesitation in making a clear choice or judgment.

Sample Sentences
She felt **ambivalent** about the job offer, as it provided a higher salary but required relocating to a new city.

His **ambivalent** feelings towards the movie were evident; he appreciated the visual effects but found the plot lacking.

Jenny's **ambivalence** towards the upcoming election stemmed from her uncertainty about the candidates' positions on key issues.

Quotes
We all have ambivalent feelings toward work ... We try to avoid it, and yet we seem to require it for our emotional well-being. *Samuel Florman*

I focus on the task and try and do it as best we can. And we're constantly evolving it, because it's my way of trying to make sense of all these ambivalent feelings I have. *Jon Stewart*

Question
What types of emotions do you usually experience when you feel ambivalent about making a big decision?

Assuage

Type: Verb

Assuage is a verb meaning to lessen the intensity of pain, distress, tension, grief, guilt, hostility, or another form of negative emotion or affliction. A useful alternative to assuage is the verb *mollify*, which shares the same meaning.

Sample Sentences

The boss's email helped to **assuage** my initial fears about joining the new team.

There is little that can be done to **assuage** the trauma and abject terror felt by a population that has witnessed war and the loss of a family member.

I hope this act of kindness can help to **assuage** the guilt I am feeling.

Quotes

I've never known any trouble than an hour's reading didn't assuage.
Arthur Schopenhauer

All the Junos, the Grammy nominations, the gold and platinum records, did nothing to assuage my conviction that I was an out-and-out loser.
Dan Hill

Question

Was there a recent issue that demanded you to act and assuage the hostility or tension?

Asymmetrical

Type: Adjective

Derived from Greek roots, the term asymmetrical literally means "not symmetrical", which is the quality or state of being uneven and lacking balance or symmetry.

When referring to a person's body type, for example, they might be asymmetrical because one arm is slightly longer than the other. There is also "asymmetrical warfare", which refers to waging war on an enemy through unconventional methods especially where the weaker force attempts to wear down the stronger force through constant harassment.

Sample Sentences

There has been much debate over whether humans are naturally symmetrical ever since the ancient Greek philosopher Aristotle contemplated the notion that symmetrical individuals were more beautiful than their **asymmetrical** counterparts.

The **asymmetrical** shape of the Echinopsis cactus is said to mimic the stinger of a honey bee.

The shirt had an unfortunate sequence of stripes, all different widths, making the shirt look **asymmetrical**.

Quotes

Differences of power are always manifested in asymmetrical access. *Marilyn Frye*

We have got to bring together the best resources in America to understand that cyber warfare is the new warfare of the asymmetrical enemies that we face in this country. *Mike Pence*

In a world where the threat is asymmetrical, where the weak defy the strong, the power of conviction, the capacity to convince, the ability to sway opinion count as much as the number of military divisions. *Dominique de Villepin*

Question

Can you think of a scenario where you might have an asymmetrical opportunity to gain more than you might lose?

Beget

Type: Verb

Beget means to procreate in the sense of having children but is more commonly used in conversation and writing to describe something that generates or brings forth more of the same.

Sample Sentences

Don't be surprised to see publicity **beget** more publicity.

With the growth of systems that recommend content on Amazon, YouTube, Spotify, and so on, more traffic **begets** more fans and exposure.

Investing revenue back into the business amplifies and begets more **revenue**.

Quotes

Change begets change. *Charles Dickens*

Violence begets violence. *Grace Lozada*

In life, success begets success. *Tim Kaine*

Question

What is an act of kindness you've recently witnessed and was there any flow-on effect? Did it beget more kindness?

Beset

Type: Verb

Beset describes a scenario where you are surrounded or set upon (assailed) by something, such as wolves, problems, controversy, etc. The use of this word dates back to the 12th Century and is often used to describe situations where someone or something is surrounded on all sides, such as a storm or army.

The other common meaning of beset is to decorate with jewels or other ornamentation, such as a crown beset with diamonds or a dress beset with silver sequins.

Sample Sentences

The brand is **beset** with controversy following its recently failed ad campaign.

You will be immediately **beset** by mosquitos if you sit there.

The world is **beset** with challenges.

Quotes

Alone, I am satisfied with myself. With others, I am beset by troubling comparisons. *Mason Cooley*

But how is the artist to protect himself against the corruption of the age which besets him on all sides? *Friedrich Schiller*

Question

If you were beset by the pressure of fame, would you thrive or would you try to hide?

Binary

Type: Adjective

Binary means something that can be broken into two categories, such as female and male, or Yes and No.

Sample Sentences

This was hardly a **binary** decision. You could have pushed for a third option.

The election represents a **binary** choice between the Democrats and Republicans.

There is a false **binary** or fallacy in society today regarding the place of politics.

Quotes

I'm a very binary person in a bad way where it's like everything is either totally great or totally awful. *Kathleen Hanna*

Any sufficiently crisp question can be answered by a single binary digit- 0 or 1, yes or no. *Carl Sagan*

Question

What binary decisions have you made today?

Byproduct

Type: Noun

When producing or developing one thing results in another thing, that second thing is called the byproduct. Muscle growth, for example, is the byproduct of lifting heavy weights.

While the byproduct has importance, it's usually secondary to the initial result or is even an unexpected consequence of the first result. In the UK, the word is generally spelled with a hyphen as *by-product*.

Sample Sentences

A major **byproduct** of the epidemic was an upswing in online communication.

Cricket and democracy were two important **byproducts** of the British Empire's occupation.

Quotes

Money and power come as a byproduct of things well done. *John Travolta*

Our customs, behaviors, and values are byproducts of our culture. *Jacque Fresco*

Mistakes are the byproduct of action - and thus an accurate gauge of effort. *Terry Rossio*

Question

What is the byproduct of investing more time in improving your vocabulary and communication skills?

Byzantine

Type: Adjective

Byzantine has numerous connotations that generally link around the idea of intricateness or complexity, and in some cases, deviousness. Byzantine is the name of the empire that had its capital city where Istanbul is today. The empire was subsumed by the Roman Republic, which resulted in difficulties regarding administration as well as a very complex and opaque government. Subsequently, the word Byzantine is now used as an adjective to describe something difficult to understand or navigate, such as a political system or a maze of roads.

Sample Sentences

We want to help customers avoid the **Byzantine** process of registering tax earnings by offering an all-in-one online submission system.

You can find yourself lost in the **Byzantine** layout of this city, which combines lanes, squares, and courts as part of one giant labyrinth.

The lifting of **Byzantine** trade restrictions helped to create new incentives for exporters and assuage the tension among trade lobbyists.

Quotes

I don't need a hard disk in my computer if I can get to the server faster... carrying around these non-connected computers is Byzantine by comparison. *Steve Jobs*

In affluent communities, where each member is keenly aware of his or her place within the Byzantine order, attracting the right friends is a blood sport. *Jamie Johnson*

Question

Is there a Byzantine procedure to submit taxes or register a business in your country?

Centers of power

Type: Noun phrase

Centers of power describes a concentration of power, such as institutions or powerful people who form a centralized coalition of authority and influence. The extent of their power usually relates to political, economic, and cultural influence.

Sample Sentences

The **centers of power** in the tech space have traditionally gravitated toward the west coast of America.

The rise of social media represented a spectacular hit to traditional media and their established **center of power**.

Washington and Moscow evolved as the **two centers of power** in the post-war era.

Quote

The danger of the Internet is cocooning with the like-minded online - of sending an email or Twitter and confusing that with action - while the real corporate and military and government centers of power go right on. *Gloria Steinem*

Question

How did the centers of power in your field or industry form and in which location?

Cinematic

Type: Adjective

Cinematic refers to something that has characteristics reminiscent of cinema/motion picture. The term cinematic is both versatile and open to interpretation as cinema consists of many forms, including film quality, acting, storyline/narrative, sound, emotions, editing, and experience. From an Instagram filter to a Hollywood storyline arch, or climactic moment, cinematic can be paired with a wide range of different nouns.

Sample Sentences
New technology delivers a sensory **cinematic** experience inside the home.

Video editing software now adds a **cinematic** polish to home movies.

Instagram offers **cinematic** filters.

Quotes
Violence is a form of cinematic entertainment. *Quentin Tarantino*

Most of us live our lives devoid of cinematic moments. *Nora Ephron*

My cinematic crush has been pretty much the same since I was 12: Kevin Costner. *Emma Watson*

Question
Is there a collection of friends, colleagues, or other acquaintances in your life that attract the dramatic ups and downs of a cinematic plot?

Circumspect

Type: Adjective

Circumspect is all about being careful, prudent, and considering different circumstances and possible consequences as a way of downsizing risk. Circumspect comes from the Latin term *circumspectus,* meaning *to be cautious.*

The word conveys a strong desire to avoid mistakes or negative consequences, which warrants the need to be hypervigilant and cautious. The word can also overlap with a feeling of dubiousness or doubt.

Sample Sentences

I was **circumspect** coming into the job, but the warm reception I received quickly helped to assuage those doubts.

As a **circumspect** observer, I was wary not to speak or act, lest I be accused of favoring one side.

Diplomacy generally calls for a fast but **circumspect** response.

Quotes

Intellectuals who live in Hungary, or who wish to work or lecture there, are extremely circumspect in their criticism. *Hari Kunzru*

My view of foreign policy is that we need to be careful and circumspect about United States intervention in any foreign nation. *Michele Bachmann*

Question

Have you come across a book title that initially made you circumspect, yet turned out to be a real page-turner?

Congruent

Type: Adjective

Congruent describes that something is similar in character or type and comes from the Latin verb *congruere*, meaning *to come together, correspond with*. Synonyms include align, consistent, and matching.

Sample Sentences

Her actions are not **congruent** with her values.

It's important that our social media posts are **congruent** with the company's mission statement.

The interior of the house was not **congruent** with its exterior appearance.

Quotes

When you are congruent in your personal life, you will be congruent in your business life. *Brendon Burchard*

The idea that we are going to be able to take our entire society as it currently works and simply change the source of energy and make it sustainable is not actually congruent with reality. *Alex Steffen*

Question

Is your current job position or field of study congruent with where you want to be in five years' time?

Conjure

Type: Verb

Conjure means to summon something into action or bring it into existence, often as if by magic. The word also means to call to mind, evoke, or imagine/picture in the mind.

Sample Sentences

Summer **conjures** up images of beaches and sunshine.

Let's see what I can **conjure** up with the limited resources available.

The story **conjures** up memories of childhood.

Quotes

It is foolish to conjure up woe where none exists. *Christopher Paolini*

When I make music, it's a very visual thing. Conjures up a lot of images. *King Krule*

Question

What ideas conjure up when you think about Christmas or another religious-themed event in your country?

Connective tissue

Type: Noun phrase

Connective tissue is a medical term explaining the tissue that fills the space and binds together other tissues, organs, tendons, and ligaments. However, connective tissue can also be used to describe the filler or glue between adjoining concepts or other aspects that connect.

Sample Sentences

Trust and friendship provided the **connective tissue** between this legendary duo.

Fiber-optic cables were invented to replace electric cables and provide a new **connective tissue** between data centers and end-users by transferring data signals in the form of light over hundreds of miles.

Community events help to grow the **connective tissue** between local citizens.

Quotes

I think that my work is my attempt, I suppose, is to try and become a piece of connective tissue. I'm trying to communicate with people here and in America - in rich countries - about what I see on the ground in badly affected areas. *Emma Thompson*

Happiness is not a noun or a verb. It's a conjunction. Connective tissue. *Eric Weiner*

Question

What's the connective tissue that holds the relationship between you and your best friend together?

Continuum

Type: Noun

Continuum refers to a sequence or progression of elements that gradually form a coherent or continuous whole, such as the four seasons.

Sample Sentences

Dust specks, meteoroids, asteroids, and planets constitute a **continuum** of sizes.

The candidate must progress through a **continuum** of challenges before reaching the final stage.

The app offers a full **continuum** of learning levels starting with absolute beginner content.

Quotes

I see litter as part of a long continuum of anti-social behavior. *Bill Bryson*

Trapped in a continuum of your own making. Awareness is the key that unlocks your opportunity for change. *Truth Devour*

There is no continuum for success. Focus on the progress, not the results. *Nick Saban*

Question

Where are you now in the continuum of life?

Corrosive

Type: Adjective

Corrosive is a substance, often a type of acid, that by a chemical reaction will eat away and destroy something (cause corrosion) if spilled or exposed to it and comes from the Latin word *corrodere*, meaning *to gnaw away*. Speaking in a more general context, corrosive simply means to destroy or irreversibly damage.

Sample Sentences
Technology is equally complementary and **corrosive** to productivity.

The work culture here is **corrosive** to happiness.

Few things are more **corrosive** to the democracy and rule of law than the combination of corruption and nepotism.

Quotes
It's such a corrosive chemical: fame. *Gertrude Berg*

Money is becoming one of the most corrosive elements of politics. *Trent Lott*

Question
What type of work environment is corrosive to productivity?

Crestfallen

Type: Adjective

Crestfallen means feeling dark, depressed, and deflated. If you feel crestfallen, you are in need of some kind words or at least a hug. While not widely known, the word is said to have evolved from a description of an animal, such as a cock, with its crested head bowed. Crest, itself, refers to the showy tuft on an animal or the plume on a knight's helmet.

Sample Sentences

I was **crestfallen** after what just happened.

I vividly remember the first time I fired someone and seeing their **crestfallen** face.

Fans were **crestfallen** after their team narrowly lost the playoff game.

Quotes

The times I didn't get jobs I wanted, I remember feeling dispirited - really crestfallen. *Jill Abramson*

Is it not true that the clever rogue is like the runner who runs well for the first half of the course, but flags before reaching the goal: he is quick off the mark, but ends in disgrace and slinks away crestfallen and uncrowned.
Plato

Question

When have you felt crestfallen?

Dichotomy

Type: Noun

A dichotomy is an idea or classification split into two sides. It's often used to refer to two mutually exclusive or contradictory/opposing ideas or groups, such as peace and war. You will also hear people talking about a *false dichotomy*, which is something that is unfairly represented as a binary either/or scenario.

Sample Sentences
There is a **dichotomy** between how the media portray the issue and what the people on the ground are saying.

To say that all hotels are either cheap and basic or expensive and luxurious creates a false **dichotomy** as some hotels don't fit into either category.

It's an unfair **dichotomy** to say that the design team and developer team have opposing and contradictory objectives.

Quotes
The great apparent dichotomy is that the more we give, the more we get. *Stephen Covey*

I want to get away from "It's either government or the market." That's a false dichotomy. *Douglas Massey*

My own career reflects a strange dichotomy between the world we've long known and the world that will become. *Jeffrey Toobin*

Question
What's an issue you often hear represented as a dichotomy? Is it a true divide or is it a false dichotomy?

Didactic

Type: Adjective

Didactic has a neutral meaning of being designed or intended to teach others but may also extend to teaching others moralistic lessons that might not be explicitly and directly requested.

Sample Sentences

By linking those **didactic** experiences, I was able to form a new interpretation of what it really means to be a parent.

The **didactic** quality of her online content helped to build a larger audience than other online lifestyle personalities.

While unfortunate, setbacks in work or relationships are often life's **didactic** humor of pushing you into action and becoming a better person.

Quotes

I do not like to be thought of as avant-garde or some kind of didactic artist. *Lucinda Childs*

A historian should not be didactic—that is a word that makes my blood run cold. *Edmund Morgan*

Question

What movie or TV show can you think of that seems like entertainment but is actually highly didactic in substance?

Efficacy

Type: Noun

Meaning the power to produce the desired effect, efficacy is a commonly used term in business, medicine, and politics as a formal way of saying "effective". Efficacy stems from the Latin verb *efficere, meaning* to work out and accomplish.

Sample Sentences
The **efficacy** of precision bombing is under question following more civilian casualties over the weekend.

There's no questioning the **efficacy** of the company's decision to open a new product line in light of the recent economic circumstances.

Clinal trials of the new drug are attempting to discern the **efficacy** in alleviating symptoms and preventing contagion.

Quotes
The power of making war often prevents it, and in our case would give efficacy to our desire of peace. *Thomas Jefferson*

I believe firmly in the efficacy of religion, in its powerful influence on a person's whole life. *Walt Disney*

The Democrats appear to be the only people who still believe there is any efficacy to the UN. *Ann Coulter*

Question
Have you considered the efficacy of learning a new skill such as computer programming or learning a second language for progressing your career?

Ensconce

Type: Verb

Meaning to fix firmly or settle for a while, the word ensconce dates to the 1580s when it meant to cover with a *fortress*, and the concept of being surrounded by all sides has endured as part of its core meaning.

Sample Sentences

From a young age, kids today are **ensconced** in the latest technology and access to on-demand entertainment.

The annual price appreciation of this stock is firmly **ensconced** in the 2-3% range.

In the video game Animal Crossing, the character Major is seen contently **ensconced** in his bed of straw.

Quotes

I spent many hours ensconced in the local library, reading - nay, devouring - book after book after book. Books were my soul's delight.
Nikki Grimes

A collective tyrant, spread over the length and breadth of the land, is no more acceptable than a single tyrant ensconced on his throne.
Georges Clemenceau

Question

Where's your favorite place to ensconce yourself when you need to get some work done?

Espouse

Type: Verb

As a verb, espouse has two meanings. Its original meaning is to get married, but the meaning has expanded to include other long-term commitments such as an important cause or belief system. Consequently, someone who lives in agreement with their specific beliefs, such as religion or environmentalism, can be said to espouse that belief system, which means to be deeply attached to a cause or belief.

Sample Sentences

I openly and committedly **espouse** the law of resting on weekends.

They do not **espouse** the same values as the general population.

The candidate's record of **espousing** progressive causes and lack of top-level experience were both contributing factors to their political downfall.

Quotes

There's room in the Republican Party for anyone who wants to be a part of the values that we espouse when it comes to the role of government, free enterprise, free markets. *Michael Steele*

One must espouse some pursuit, taking it kindly at heart and with enthusiasm. *Amos Bronson Alcott*

There are only two distinct classes of people on this earth, those who espouse enthusiasm and those who despise it. *Madame de Stael*

Question

What values or belief systems do you espouse as a result of your parents or childhood upbringing?

Ethereal

Type: Adjective

Ethereal describes something intangible, light, or airy, such as an ethereal sense of design or beauty. Ethereal comes from the Greek word *ether,* meaning *air,* and *the upper regions of space.* The word, therefore, usually refers to things beyond the earth and having an almost supernatural or heavenly quality. The word can also be used to describe something delicate and light, like the sound of a singer's voice.

Sample Sentences
The phone's design exudes an **ethereal** feeling of weightlessness.

The film captures an **ethereal** sense of nostalgic longing for faded glory.

The baker promised an **ethereal** taste for the royal wedding cake.

Quotes
Music is truly love itself, the purest, most ethereal language of the emotions, embodying all their changing colors in every variety of shading and nuance. *Carl Maria von Weber*

Willpower is concrete, not ethereal. When you do something, you demonstrate your willpower, and it becomes all the easier to have the same power of will the next time. *B.K.S. Iyengar*

Question
Is there a person that comes to mind who you might describe as ethereal? Is it the way they speak and carry themselves? Or was it something they were wearing that one night?

Facetious

Type: Adjective

This is a useful adjective for talking about something you shouldn't take seriously. Facetious comes from the French word *facétie*, meaning *joke*, and has come to imply a joke that is witty but contains some element of sarcasm and should not be taken seriously. The word may also imply that someone is being inappropriately funny about a serious topic.

If you forget how to spell facetious, remember that it contains all five vowels in alphabetical order.

Sample Sentences

If you've just won a hotdog-eating contest and your friend asks if you'd like to go out for burgers, they're probably being **facetious**.

It was meant to be a **facetious** suggestion, not something you should take seriously.

The celebrity's **facetious** Facebook post quickly made its rounds with the major media outlets, who accused the star of trivializing the broader issue.

Quote

I am not being facetious when I say that the real enemies in this country are the Pentagon and its pals in big business. *Bella Abzug*

Question

Have you ever been accused by a parent or teacher of being facetious?

Flippant

Type: Adjective

Flippant means lacking proper respect or seriousness. Carrying a negative undertone, flippant is often used to describe a blasé and inappropriate attitude or comment in a situation that requires more seriousness.

Sample Sentences
Her **flippant** remark about the crisis was deemed insensitive by many.

The CEO was **flippant** that the employee boycott would harm the company's longstanding position of leadership in the apparel market.

The stereotypes and **flippant** treatment of the elderly on TV have negative repercussions on the mental health of senior citizens in our society.

Quotes
The public's appetite for frothy, flippant blondes has waned, but Paris Hilton still fascinates me. *Diablo Cody*

It is not a mark of manhood to carelessly use the name of the Almighty or of His Beloved Son in a vain and flippant way, as many are prone to do. *Gordon B. Hinckley*

Question
Is there a politician you can think of who is said to be inappropriate and flippant in their behavior?

Fodder

Type: Noun

Fodder is cheap food, usually given to livestock animals such as cows, horses, and sheep. The word is not just limited to animal food, fodder can also describe inferior or readily available material that is used for a particular purpose or to supply heavy demand.

Sample Sentences

The celebrity marriage and divorce cycle in L.A. provides endless **fodder** for the paparazzi.

Young and underemployed viewers on YouTube provide easy **fodder** for fake gurus to sell their expensive courses.

Expendable in the face of enemy fire, soldiers are sometimes used as cannon **fodder** by their government or military command in order to win some other tacit objective.

Quotes

One of the ways I think I gain fodder for characters is by watching people. *Edie Falco*

Hypocrisy is great fodder for comedy. *Mo Rocca*

Question

What kind of experiences or situations serve as the best fodder for funny stories?

Frivolous

Type: Adjective

Frivolous refers to being unnecessary or even silly. The word is often used to describe something that has no substantial value or is wasteful, such as a frivolous lawsuit that wastes the court's time or a frivolous acquisition of another company.

Sample Sentences

The President's lawyer contends that the lawsuit is **frivolous** and should not be taken seriously.

The internal company survey produced nothing but **frivolous** complaints.

If I want my dose of **frivolous** gossip, I know who to talk to.

I think he was being overly **frivolous** with his praise for the project when he should have been focusing on other matters.

Quotes

Fashion is not frivolous. *Donatella Versace*

Frivolous sorrow is folly. Frivolous enjoyment is not. *Mason Cooley*

Do not be frivolous with the gift of a day. Right now, it's all you have. Yesterday is history. *Robert Genn*

Question

Who in your life would you point to as a frivolous spender?

Fungible

Type: Adjective

Fungible is used to describe something that is interchangeable or easily substituted, such as a commodity. This means that no matter which unit of the product you have, it is considered the same. For example, a one-hundred-dollar note is equivalent to any other because they are identical in value. Handmade art, on the other hand, is less fungible as there is a difference in the quality and value between one art piece and another.

Sample Sentences
In the financial market, stocks are considered **fungible** assets.

If you inherit a locket from your grandmother, its sentimental value will be hard to measure. However, if you buy a generic gold-plated pendant, it can be considered a **fungible** possession.

Until recently, digital artworks were **fungible**, since they could be copied and reused for different purposes without any consequences. This has now changed with the introduction of blockchain technology and non-fungible tokens, known as NFTs.

Quotes
Capital in money form has no citizenship. It is fungible, an asset capable of moving from place to place in a nanosecond. *Eric Kierans*

Realistically, it's the great truism that screenwriters are fungible, that at the end of the day a studio is not going to want to fire a movie star. *John Logan*

Question
What assets do you have that would be considered fungible?

Haphazard

Type: Adjective

Haphazard describes something marked by a lack of planning, order, or direction. Something that is haphazard is thus likely to be random, hit-or-miss, or unpredictable, and generally not a situation or something to aspire to—as hazard, after all, refers to danger.

Interestingly, the prefix "hap" in "haphazard" comes from the English word *happening*, which comes from the Old Norse word *happ,* meaning *good luck.* Consequently, haphazard originally came into the English language as a noun meaning *chance* in the 16th Century before evolving into an adjective to describe something with no apparent order or logic. You can still find remnants of its original use case in the form of "I'll hazard a guess," which means *I'll take a chance at guessing.*

Sample Sentences

The project was **haphazard** from start to finish.

The camp was erected **haphazardly** in a matter of hours.

Japan's **haphazard** policy response following the disaster did little to assuage public concerns and their diminishing faith in the government.

Quotes

My so-called career is a haphazard thing. *Paul McCartney*

Most writers write haphazardly. The actor is fighting unjustified words all the time. *Marlon Brando*

The country is laid out in a haphazard, sloppy fashion, offensive to the tidy, organized mind. *Alan Brien*

Question

Is there a company you can think of that constantly bumps into one crisis after another and which you might describe as a haphazard operation?

Happy medium

Type: Noun phrase

A happy medium is a good choice or a condition that avoids any one extreme. This term is valuable as it avoids the negative implication of compromise, instead highlighting the fertile middle ground achieved between multiple extremes.

Sample Sentences

The car's designers wanted to strike a **happy medium** between affordability and luxury.

I have struck a **happy medium** in my career where I no longer need to resort to alcohol or large dinners to close big deals.

My partner and I have found a **happy medium** in our relationship in which we no longer bicker over minor issues.

Quotes

There must be a happy medium somewhere between being totally informed and blissfully unaware. *Doug Larson*

Greece is not a country of happy mediums: everything there seems to be either wonderful or horrible ... *Nancy Mitford*

Question

What if instead, you internalized the next sacrifice as striking a happy medium? How would that serve you and/or your relationship with that person?

Incorruptible

Type: Adjective

Opposite to corrupt, incorruptible is someone or something that cannot be bribed, morally corrupted, or subject to decay. Someone who is honest is incorruptible.

Sample Sentences

An inclusive work environment is grounded in the genuine and **incorruptible** acceptance of other people.

New Yorkers are known for their **incorruptible** spirit to work hard and overcome adversity.

My moral position on this issue is **incorruptible** and immune to change.

Quotes

Does advertising corrupt editors? Yes it does, but fewer editors than you may suppose... the vast majority of editors are incorruptible. *David Ogilvy*

My characters are driven by a passionate desire for justice. They are rebellious and incorruptible. *Tahar Ben Jelloun*

Question

Is there someone in your family or social network who has incorruptible integrity?

Ineffable

Type: Adjective

Counter to the theme of this book, ineffable means something that cannot be expressed in words. It usually refers to something that is unspeakably beautiful, touching, or horrible, and therefore beyond expression or difficult to put into words. While no longer widely used, the base word "effable" is also an adjective meaning something that can lawfully be expressed in words.

Sample Sentences
Parents might experience an **ineffable** sense of sadness and pride when dropping off their child at school for the first time.

Despite the overwhelming sadness, he found solace in the **ineffable** awe and transcendental experience of walking alone in nature.

Bleak and dreary, the weather left me in an **ineffable** mood.

Quotes
To become aware of the ineffable is to part company with words. *Abraham Joshua Heschel*

Renunciation made for the sake of service is an ineffable joy of which none can deprive anyone, because that nectar springs from within and sustains life. *Mahatma Gandhi*

Lovers have an ineffable instinct which detects the presence of rivals. *Henry Bulwer*

Question
What environment gives you an ineffable feeling of belonging and satisfaction?

Inhabit

Type: Verb

To inhabit is to occupy a physical place such as a settled residence or to be present in any manner of form. The first use case of this verb—in regard to physical positioning—is simple. You can say the dog inhabits one part of the house, previous generations inhabited caves, or the Earth inhabits the Solar System. The second use case is more abstract in meaning and may refer to ideas that inhabit the mind or inhabit the personality of someone else.

Inhabit comes from Old French, *enhabiter*, meaning *to dwell in*.

Sample Sentences

Stress and external pressure can easily cascade to **inhabit** the mind and obscure clear judgment of the situation.

This island is no longer **inhabited**.

She **inhabits** a world of her own making, sometimes untethered from the reality of modern life.

Quotes

Friendship is two souls inhabiting one body. *Aristotle*

We inhabit a universe that is still inventing itself. *Peter Corning*

I just like to inhabit a character really deeply. *Curtis Sittenfeld*

Question

Would you consider inhabiting another planet such as Mars?

Inhibit

Type: Verb

Inhibit is a verb meaning to hinder, restrain, or limit. This might entail using physical force or the power of authority to stop the spread of something, or it may refer to a belief that is limiting your potential.

Sample Sentences

Scarcity and seeing things in short supply is an **inhibiting** mindset.

The delayed response from the government did little to **inhibit** the spread of the virus.

The drug is designed to **inhibit** the growth of cancer cells.

Quotes

You can't accomplish anything worthwhile if you inhibit yourself. *Oprah Winfrey*

When we point to obstacles we inhibit progress. When we offer solutions we advance. *Simon Sinek*

Question

What is currently inhibiting your progress? Why is it inhibiting you?

Interoperable

Type: Adjective

Interoperable is an adjective that describes systems or organizations that can exchange data and use the same standards. The opposite of interoperable is *proprietary*, i.e., when something is only compatible with certain products from one company and not with another company's, even though they typically serve the same purpose (e.g., operating systems: Windows vs. Linux).

Note that interoperable doesn't just relate to software services, it can include hardware as well. Its noun version, *interoperability*, is also common in usage.

Sample Sentences

Our **interoperable** systems enable different actors to work together by exchanging information according to agreed-upon rules and procedures. This supports the sharing of resources and knowledge among different service providers in an open environment.

Beyond the barriers of **interoperability** across digital platforms and operating systems, there is also the challenge of technology adoption, which has been much maligned throughout the history of virtual reality.

The new software is designed to provide payment **interoperability** between banks and other providers.

Question

Have you come across any interoperability barriers between your systems, devices, or hardware, such as syncing problems or compatibility issues?

Intuit

Type: Verb

Similar to a hunch, intuit means using your intuition to get a strong sense of something. The word comes from the Latin root *intueri*, meaning to look at, comprehend, or contemplate.

Sample Sentences

Children have an uncanny ability to **intuit** and read adult behavior.

This teacher **intuited** that I was having trouble and offered me extra help.

It's difficult to **intuit** what humans might eventually do with this new technology.

Quotes

If you can intuit well, you're essentially meeting the future faster. *Peter Buffett*

Bring the mind to a sharp focus and make it alert so that it can immediately intuit truth, which is everywhere. *Bruce Lee*

Question

What information can you intuit about a person based on what they wear?

Jarring

Type: Adjective

Jarring has several meanings that revolve around the idea of a sudden jolt or happening. This could be a loud and sudden sound, a physical vibration or knock, or a shocking piece of news, for example.

Sample Sentences
The contrast between the film's plot and the original novel was **jarring**.

Hitting pause on a promising vaccine due to bureaucratic restraints is **jarring**, especially during a deadly pandemic.

I'd grown up seeing people wear masks on the streets of Hong Kong, but it felt **jarring** to see people wearing them here in suburban America.

Quotes
My favorite books, art pieces, films, and music, always have something jarring about them. *Pink*

It's almost jarring when you go to play a different character, after playing someone for so long. I love it! *Bridget Regan*

Question
Have you ever experienced a jarring tackle or a jarring injury?

Jettison

Type: Verb

Jettison means to push to the side or release. If a ship is leaking or a jet is running out of fuel, you can buy time by jettisoning cargo to reduce the weight. Beyond physically throwing something away, you can also use jettison to describe breaking ties with a person, belief, or another abstract subject.

Sample Sentences

Few people questioned the Supreme Court's decision to **jettison** their original order.

We need to **jettison** the notion that cooperation in this industry is a zero-sum game.

The team is likely to **jettison** the disgraced player at the end of the season.

Quotes

Television, as you know, can kind of jettison you into a whole new world. *David Caruso*

During the great storms of our lives we imitate those captains who jettison their weightiest cargo. *Honore de Balzac*

Question

Is there a relationship or a commitment in your life that you've been holding off from letting go of or permanently jettisoning?

Junket

Type: Noun or verb

A junket is a trip taken for pleasure and funded by someone else. In the case of a government official, the cost is covered at public expense (taxpayers' money). Despite the official rationale for taking the trip, junkets are generally treated as a pleasure trip or fancy holiday (i.e. staying at a nice resort) or supplied as a gift to someone in order to extract a favor, such as a travel reporter who is invited by a resort owner to stay at their new property, with the expectation that they will provide a positive write-up. While junket can be used as a verb, it's most often used as a noun.

Sample Sentences
The first day of the auto show is usually reserved for press events, drawing many journalists who are quick to sign up for the annual **junket**.

The congressional **junket** was eventually exposed by the press.

Quote
I guess I kind of realized that my whole life isn't one giant press junket. I don't have to be smiling all the time and always have the perfect answer. *Miley Cyrus*

Question
Which professions today are most likely to authorize junkets for their employees?

Laconic

Type: Adjective

Laconic is an adjective that describes a concise way of speaking. To be a laconic speaker means to be brief and to use a minimum number of words. It may also mean being concise to the point of seeming rude or brunt, and can therefore carry a negative connotation. Interestingly, the word comes from Laconia (Sparta), a region in ancient Greece where the local rulers gave very short speeches.

Sample Sentences
He always talks in a very methodical and **laconic** manner.

His **laconic** baritone did little to cut through the background ambiance.

My father was always a dry and **laconic** storyteller.

Quotes
Those of you who have spent time with Australians know that we are not given to overstatement. By nature, we are laconic speakers and by conviction we are realistic thinkers. *Julia Gillard*

You can get far in North America with laconic grunts. "Huh," "hun," and "hi!" in their various modulations, together with "sure," "guess so," "that so?" and "nuts!" will meet almost any contingency. *Ian Fleming*

Question
Who in your network would make a good Spartan ruler given their economic use of words?

Loquacious

Type: Adjective

The opposite of laconic is loquacious, which means a person who talks excessively, often about topics only they think are interesting.

Sample Sentences

For most people, a **loquacious** person is not someone you want to sit next to on a long overnight flight.

The young Senator was known to be **loquacious** and boastful.

I definitely err towards laconic on the spectrum of **loquaciousness**.

Quotes

We should not expect the state to appear in the guise of an extravagant good fairy at every christening, a loquacious companion at every stage of life's journey, and the unknown mourner at every funeral. *Margaret Thatcher*

I'm probably the most loquacious author when it comes to my dedications. *Karen Kingsbury*

Question

Are there any situations or environments where one may describe you as being loquacious?

Luddite

Type: Noun

Luddite is a noun used to describe people who dislike the use of new technology, particularly when they feel like it threatens their job security. For example, if someone's work became obsolete because of advances in technology, they might become a Luddite.

The word comes from an early 19th-century English movement that opposed labor-saving machinery, especially in the textile industry. The group was named after its semi-mythical leader Ned Ludd.

Sample Sentences

The **Luddite** approach of resisting technological change can be harmful to future employment opportunities.

The company is full of **Luddite** employees with little vision of how the future of the industry will evolve.

Quotes

I don't have a computer. I am the Luddite of rock'n'roll, I don't have a portable phone. I write things down. *Elton John*

I'm a Luddite with computers, and I'm slightly worried about being hacked as well. *Jo Brand*

Question

Do you usually embrace new technology, or would you describe yourself as a technological Luddite?

Magnify

Type: Verb

To magnify is to make something bigger in size or significance. This is a verb you've heard and maybe used before but deserves special attention. The strength of this word is its familiarity; as a kid, you probably used a magnifying glass to look at stamps, terrorize ants, or antagonize an older or younger sibling. This makes magnify an easy word to imagine and visualize, which in turn, brings emphasis and vividness to your writing or speech. Tony Robbins, a great exponent of natural language processing, uses the word magnify frequently to explain money, relationships, and other important life matters.

Sample Sentences

Remaining in this home without him will only **magnify** the pain.

The press **magnified** the problem by making it into a bigger story than it actually was.

This month's poor sales report **magnified** the need to hire a new sales team.

Quotes

"Money doesn't change people. It just magnifies who they already are: if you have a lot of money and you're mean, then you have more to be mean with; if you have a lot of money and you're generous, you'll naturally give more." *Tony Robbins*

Magnify the virtues, minimize the faults. *Edgar Cayce*

Question

What can you do today to magnify your overall happiness?

Maim

Type: Verb

To maim means to hurt or disfigure through force or violence. The word relates to mayhem, which in the past described the act of hurting another person or animal badly. These days, maim is often used to describe types of attacks that involve the loss of a limb.

Sample Sentences
The recent algorithm update on Amazon has **maimed** our daily sales.

The 18-year-old vigilante was sentenced for murder and **maiming** a second victim.

The car accident left my classmate horrifically **maimed.**

Quotes
What molds us is what maims us. *Dennis Lehane*

In football, you can always maim a person if you wanted to. *Lawrence Taylor*

Question
What types of animals are known for maiming humans?

Malleable

Type: Adjective

Derived from the Medieval Latin term *malleābilis, to hammer,* malleable describes a metal that can be pounded or pressed into various shapes. It can also be used to express that something is workable, that it can be changed or reshaped, such as someone's view and interpretation of the world.

Sample Sentences

Culture is **malleable** and evolves with each passing generation.

It's easier to learn a language when you're young and **malleable**.

Reputation is not a fixed entity but rather something that is **malleable** and open to change.

Quotes

Rock is much more malleable than ideas. *Kim Stanley Robinson*

Habits are malleable throughout your entire life. *Charles Duhigg*

We all have memories that are malleable and susceptible to being contaminated or supplemented in some way. *Elizabeth Loftus*

The world is a very malleable place. If you know what you want, and you go for it with maximum energy and drive and passion, the world will often reconfigure itself around you much more quickly and easily than you would think. *Marc Andreessen*

Question

How malleable are you to external feedback? Is there a way for you to be more malleable in order to develop yourself professionally?

Masquerade

Type: Verb and noun

Masquerade has two use cases. As a noun, masquerade describes a social gathering of people wearing masks and fancy costumes. Note that it may also refer directly to the (masquerade) mask. As a verb, it can mean to disguise oneself or pretend to be someone else.

Sample Sentences

In the Disney movie *Mulan*, the female protagonist **masquerades** as a man. (verb)

The company is ensconced in an ego war **masquerading** as a boardroom division. (verb)

He liked to **masquerade** as a food critic to get free samples at restaurants. (verb)

Last week's **masquerade** ball was said to be a decadent affair. (noun)

Quotes

Precise forecasts masquerade as accurate ones. *Nate Silver*

The good don't masquerade their goodness, they just are. *Innocent Mwatsikesimbe*

Question
Have you ever masqueraded as someone you're not? What disguises did you employ?

Misappropriate

Type: Verb

Misappropriate is a verb meaning to dishonestly take something, such as money or an identity, for personal use. Misappropriate combines the prefix "mis", meaning *bad* or *wrong*, and "appropriate", which is to take possession of something. When you misappropriate something, you are usually committing theft or embezzlement—to use something in a way its owner didn't intend.

The word is often used in legal prose to describe the theft of funds within a company. You might hear the phrase "to misappropriate funds" on the news to describe someone who has used access to money in their company to commit theft.

Sample Sentences

It is unethical and illegal to **misappropriate** someone else's creative work without proper attribution.

A number of accusations were leveled at the banker, who was dismissed for allegedly **misappropriating** funds by paying himself a bonus and donating funds to a relative's charity.

The **misappropriation** of a trademark name or logo is a serious offense in many states.

Quotes

Everything's stolen. Everything precious - be it a kiss, or be it James Brown - gets misappropriated to the aid of the advertising executives. So, an act of reclamation, somewhere else to be: that's what I want my music to be. Somewhere you can step into. A place. *David Gray*

The misappropriation of resources provided by the government for weapons means the Nigerian military is unable to beat Boko Haram. *Muhammadu Buhari*

Question

Aside from money, what else might people be tempted to misappropriate from their employer or place of work?

Myopic

Type: Adjective

Myopic is an adjective meaning shortsighted and limited in physical sight or attention. In medicine, it means to be unable to clearly see objects that are far away. Meanwhile, in a more general sense, myopic expresses a focus on things that are happening currently or that relate to a particular subject area rather than thinking about the future or thinking more broadly and holistically.

Sample Sentences
The company's **myopic** approach neglected potential future challenges.

While it is sometimes good to focus narrowly on a particular research area, one's understanding of that field is also at risk of becoming **myopic** without understanding the broader implications and neighboring fields of research.

Football was a **myopic** obsession for me during my childhood. If it wasn't related to football, it didn't matter.

Quotes
I don't do the L.A. scene. I stay focused and very myopic. I don't feel I need to prove myself or be in people's faces, especially in this town. *Taylor Kitsch*

I think people tend to be very myopic and they don't understand how their actions impact others. *Jen Lancaster*

Question
In what period of your life were you most myopic in your interests or general attention?

Myriad

Type: Noun or adjective

Myriad expresses the meaning of innumerable or a great number of. Myriad comes from *myrioi*, the Greek word for ten thousand. Myriad can be a noun, i.e. a myriad of restaurant options, or an adjective, i.e. myriad patterns.

Sample Sentences
While it might sound cliché, it is true; love works in a **myriad** of ways. (noun)

Exploring the vast ocean revealed a **myriad** of marine creatures, from colorful fish to intricate coral formations. (noun)

The court found **myriad** examples of nepotism, corruption, and a penchant for fine wines. (adjective)

Quotes
In a myriad of ways you tell one truth. *Dejan Stojanovic*

Love covers a myriad of plausibility structures. *Carol Plum Ucci*

Every second that you're filming, you have a myriad of choices to make. *Anne Makepeace*

Question
In what aspect of your life are you confronted with a myriad of choices?

Neophobia

Type: Noun

Neophobia is the fear or dislike of anything new and unfamiliar. The word can also be used to describe an unwillingness to try new things or break from routine. In the context of children, the term is often used to describe kids who reject unknown or untried types of food.

This term tends to pop up more in academic writing than in general conversation. Therefore, you may need to provide some context when using this word, i.e. "I hate new things. I am neophobic at heart." In this example, the audience can detect the meaning of neophobic by the context of the previous sentence.

Sample Sentences

Studies show that **neophobia** towards eating novel foods tends to be more pronounced in young children than in adolescents.

Neophobia prevented me from trying any exotic cuisine on my vacation.

It's difficult to distinguish whether the source of the problem is poor product-market fit or just general **neophobia** regarding new technology.

Question

Is there a person in your network that you could describe as neophobic? Why?

Nominal

Type: Adjective

This word has several meanings in English, including the rate of interest (in financial terms), as well as in name only, and being trifling or insignificant in amount.

As an adjective, nominal can describe a very small or insignificant amount such as a nominal donation to a good cause or a nominal supply of resources. As a noun, nominal typically refers to something that exists in name only but perhaps not in reality, such as nominal authority over a pet who neither obeys nor listens!

Sample Sentences

My generous job title was **nominal** and not an accurate reflection or description of my actual position in the company.

Contrary to centralized finance, where the control over funds and transactions belongs **nominally** to customers, decentralized finance deconstructs this centralized model and instead distributes it across all actors.

At some stage, you will probably be charged a **nominal** amount to your bank card in order to complete online user verification.

Quotes

The nominal budget is a poor indicator of the impact of government outlays and revenues. *William Vickrey*

Nominally, there is one executive for every eight federal employees, a ratio that would bankrupt many private industries. *Martin L. Gross*

My mother was an unbeliever - and still is. My father was a nominal Catholic. We would go in to church at the last minute before the gospel reading, take Communion, and walk right out again. *Frederica Mathewes-Green*

Question

What are the advantages of charging a nominal fee for a software service compared to offering it for free?

Nepotism

Type: Noun

Nepotism is the practice among people with power or influence of favoring relatives or friends over those who are not family or friends; usually by giving them jobs or positions of authority. While it's often used in reference to companies and governments, nepotism can also take place in sports, schools, churches, and many other places where there are limited positions of power or privilege.

Sample Sentences
The company has received numerous complaints of **nepotism** regarding its hiring practices.

Nepotism is rife in this university.

Avoiding **nepotism** and special treatment is difficult when you are coaching a team that contains one or more family members.

Quotes
Nepotism sometimes can be a lose-lose situation. *Vikram Chatwal*

I made nepotism an art form, so I get to work with a lot of relatives and they're part of it. *Garry Marshall*

Yeah, my real name is Coppola. I changed it because they'd think I was some nepotism-oriented kid. *Nicolas Cage*

Question
What's an institution or company that comes to mind when you think of the word nepotism?

Obscure

Type: Verb or adjective

Obscure comes from Latin *obscurus*, meaning dark, unclear, humble, or insignificant, and is often used as an adjective to describe something vague, hard to find, or not easily understood. It can also be used as a verb in the sense of concealing or hiding. For instance, the new building across the street obscures our oceanfront view.

Sample Sentences

Our aim is to bring this information to the masses rather than keep it under lock and key somewhere in the academic world and **obscure** journals. (adjective)

What I like most about Japan is not Tokyo or Kyoto but the **obscure** villages you would be hard-pressed to spot on any tourist map. (adjective)

Don't let the past **obscure** your judgment. (verb)

Quotes

Facts can obscure the truth. *Maya Angelou*

In laboring to be concise, I become obscure. *Horace*

The more obscure our tastes, the greater the proof of our genius. *Jennifer Donnelly*

Question

Is there an obscure book or blog post that you've read recently?

Orbit

Type: Noun or verb

Orbit describes a circular path. While it's often used to talk about the revolution of the earth around the sun and other elliptical movements around a central body, orbit can also be used abstractly to describe interpersonal or other relationships (that revolve around someone/something).

Sample Sentences
This person comes in and out of our social **orbit** depending on whether they need a favor from someone in the group. (noun)

The party was filled with a constant stream of individuals vying for attention, **orbiting** around the celebrity in hopes of catching a moment of their spotlight. (verb)

Living in the **orbit** of goal-driven people has helped me to grow my business. (noun)

Quote
Sometimes you can't realize you're in a bad mood until another person enters your orbit. *Douglas Coupland*

Question
How can you get into the orbit of the rich and famous?

Parlay

Type: Verb

Parlay means to turn initial winnings from a previous bet into a greater amount by gambling. In a business context, parlay means to reinvest or take initial profits to grow business profits further.

Sample Sentences

My friend quickly **parlayed** the invitation for a coffee into an invitation to drive my new car.

I'm hoping to **parlay** my time with Google into a career in consulting.

The plan is to **parlay** the initial profits into further advertising campaigns.

Quote

I thought if I could do stand-up comedy well enough, I could parlay it back into films - like Charlie Chaplin and Woody Allen did. *Mike Birbiglia*

Question

How can you parlay your gained knowledge and experience in your current industry or field of study into another?

Passé

Type: Adjective

Meaning to have passed its time of use or usefulness, passé carries a negative connotation of faded glory. While once well-thought-of as popular, the word means that something is now out-of-date and comes from the French word *passer, to pass.*

Sample Sentences

The style is now rather **passé**, wouldn't you say?

Honestly, I think distinct celebrity baby names are becoming **passé**.

This style was once in vogue but is now considered **passé.**

Quote

It's very passé to think women want to spend a fortune on clothes.
Tory Burch

Question

What is popular today that will soon become passé in the future?

Plurality

Type: Noun

Plurality is the state of being plural, which means being numerous or of a large and undefined number. The word tends to describe non-physical concepts such as languages, ideas, races, votes, etc., rather than physical items such as trees and books.

Sample Sentences

The United States is a nation containing a **plurality** of races and religions.

In a company board election with three or more candidates where no one receives more than half of the votes, one candidate can win if they have the **plurality**.

Although official languages are very important in the definition and representation of a country, the **plurality** of local languages should be embraced and preserved.

Quotes

What is certain is that plurality and diversity are not, and never can be, a natural 'byproduct' of unregulated market forces. *David Puttnam*

Nixon's full term was one of the most successful in U.S. history, which is why he was re-elected by the largest plurality in the country's history. *Conrad Black*

Question

Let's say you wanted an environment where you could expose yourself to a plurality of contrarian ideas on a given subject, where might that place be? Would it be the library or a university club, for example, or maybe an online forum like Reddit?

Platonic

Type: Adjective

Platonic describes a relationship that is purely spiritual or intimate and marked by the absence of romance or sex. Platonic refers to the ancient Greek philosopher, Plato, who wrote on the subject of love. While Plato acknowledged physical desire, he believed that if two people inspired each other, their spiritual love would bring them closer to God.

Example

They are just a guy and a girl who spend a lot of time together; their relationship is more of a **platonic** friendship contrary to what others might say.

The mentorship between the seasoned artist and the aspiring painter was purely **platonic**, focusing on artistic guidance and inspiration without any romantic intentions.

Jane and Mark shared a deep and **platonic** friendship that had lasted for years, built on mutual respect and common interests.

Quotes

Platonic friendship—the interval between the introduction and the first kiss. *Sophie Irene Loeb*

Harry and Hermione are very platonic friends. But I won't answer for anyone else, nudge-nudge wink-wink! *J. K. Rowling*

Question

Do you have a platonic relationship with someone at work, school, or some other setting?

Polychromatic

Type: Adjective

Polychromatic is an adjective that refers to something having a variety of colors. It usually describes objects, artworks, or displays that exhibit a wide range of hues or shades.

Sample Sentences

For a **polychromatic** view of the city, I recommend sneaking up to the top floor—just before dusk, when daylight fades into darkness—to watch the skyline and horizon transform.

The artist's vibrant and **polychromatic** masterpiece filled the gallery with a mesmerizing display of colors that seemed to dance across the canvas.

The garden was a riot of **polychromatic** blooms, ranging from deep red roses to brilliant yellow daisies, creating a stunning visual spectacle.

Question

Do you remember a time when you saw a car or truck with a polychromatic exterior?

Penchant

Type: Noun

Penchant is a strong preference, tendency, or natural inclination for something. The word comes from the French word *pencher,* meaning *to incline*. Note that this word usually refers to desires.

Sample Sentences
People living in this part of China have a **penchant** for green tea.

This president has a **penchant** for pardoning friends who run afoul of the law.

My colleague has a **penchant** for saying too much.

Quotes
Americans have a penchant for the future and tend to disregard the past. *Alan Dundes*

I always had a penchant for falling in love. Every time I found myself without a mate, I fell into a state of low-sizzling panic. *Jane Fonda*

Question
What type of wine do you like? Do you have a penchant for expensive labels?

Pensive

Type: Adjective

Pensive comes from the Spanish verb *pensar* meaning *to think*. Pensiveness is characterized by the absence of any facial expression or frowning as a result of being engrossed in deep thought. Note that pensiveness doesn't always describe sad thoughtfulness, rather, it could also be that someone is simply lost in thought.

Sample Sentences
I was in a **pensive** mood all afternoon after receiving her message.

You had a **pensive** expression on your face, so I wanted to check to see if everything is okay.

The mood here is still and **pensive** since he left.

Quotes
Everyone looked pensive, which is good cover-up for clueless. *Nelson DeMille*

He was imposing, even in his pensiveness. *George Barr McCutcheon*

Question
Who in your life might you describe as a pensive personality?

Posit

Type: Verb

Posit is a verb that means to assume, propose, or put forward something as a fact, argument, or hypothesis without necessarily providing concrete evidence or proof. It's often used when discussing ideas or concepts that are being suggested or considered for further exploration or discussion.

Sample Sentences

The author used the novel as a platform to **posit** a thought-provoking question: What if technology reached a point where it could simulate human emotions indistinguishably?

The research team **posits** that there's a limit to how much consumers will spend on non-essential items this year.

I **posit** there will be great changes this year to the way we view the bilateral relationship.

Quotes

To posit the existence of a Creator requires only reason. To posit the existence of a good God requires faith. *Dennis Prager*

Some international relations scholars would posit that interest in zombies is an indirect attempt to get a cognitive grip on what U.S. Secretary of Defense Donald Rumsfeld famously referred to as the "unknown knowns" in international security. *Daniel Drezner*

Question

What do you posit your friends will say if you quit your job to pursue an ambitious life dream?

Preamble

Type: Noun

Preamble is an explanatory statement indicating what is to follow. While not always required, a preamble is often used in formal documents, such as a national constitution, with the purpose of indicating the background, history, and intent of a document, resolving any potential ambiguities about the said document. A preamble should not be confused with a document's introduction, prologue, epilogue, or summary.

Preamble comes from the Middle French word *preambule* and the Medieval Latin word *preambulum*, meaning *to walk in front of*.

Sample Sentences

This podcast has far less **preamble** than other podcasts, which saves me from skipping the first few minutes of each episode.

The school's Principal spent almost as much time on his **preamble** as he did on the actual address to parents regarding the issue of student safety.

The speaker began their presentation with a thoughtful **preamble**, providing context and background information to help the audience become better acquainted with the topic.

Quotes

The preamble of thought, the transition through which it passes from the unconscious to the conscious, is action. *Ralph Waldo Emerson*

Their political ideal set in the preamble of the Constitution affirms a life of liberty, equality and fraternity. *B. R. Ambedkar*

Question

What are some of the benefits of including a preamble in an official document or presentation?

Predicate

Type: Verb or noun

Used as a verb, predicate means to require something as a condition of something else and is pronounced *pre-duh-kate*. As a noun, predicate means the part of a sentence or clause that expresses what is said of the subject and is pronounced *pred-uh-kit*.

The example sentences below focus on the verb variant, which is usually paired with "on" to describe a connection in logic, rhetoric, economics, or another form of assumed evidence.

Sample Sentences

My decision to quit was **predicated** on the stress my job was bringing to my health.

Free markets are **predicated** on greed.

The acquisition was **predicated** on Facebook's fears of competition rather than genuine business integration.

Quotes

Value investing is predicated on the efficient market hypothesis being wrong. *Seth Klarman*

Advertising in the past has been predicated on a mass market and a captive audience. *Howard Rheingold*

Question

For what reason did you predicate your decision to leave your last job?

Primordial

Type: Adjective

Primordial is a scientific term to describe that something has existed or persisted since the earliest time, i.e., the beginning of the universe. As an adjective, it can also be used to describe an innate quality that has always existed, such as a human urge or a type of behavior.

Sample Sentences

After so many days in quarantine, I was filled with a **primordial** urge to step outside and talk to other people.

Love is a **primordial** emotion. Everyone needs it and is searching for it.

The language of cavemen was **primordial** and consisted of only a few words.

According to the Bible, life began with the **primordial** creation of Adam and Eve.

Quotes

The man who speaks with primordial images, speaks with a thousand tongues. *Carl Jung*

Every war casts humanity back into the primordial slime. *Marty Rubin*

Question

Jeff Bezos built a business model at Amazon knowing that people's propensity for lower prices would never change. What's another primordial urge that doesn't change and influences what we are willing to buy?

Propensity

Type: Noun

Propensity means a natural tendency to behave in a certain way. Everyone has their own propensities or behavioral inclinations. Similar words include innate, tendency, and penchant.

Sample Sentences

Young children have a **propensity** to touch things they shouldn't.

Some people have a **propensity** to eat too much.

Amazon customers have a **propensity** to click on "Also Boughts".

Algorithms have a powerful **propensity** to encode human behavior and reflect our own biases.

Quotes

I have this propensity to just come out and say things. That's how I am in real life. *Miguel*

I have a natural propensity to work on big piles of poop. *Robert Pattinson*

We have all a propensity to grasp at forbidden fruit. *Ralph Cudworth*

Question

What was your natural propensity as a child?

Pseudonym

Type: Noun

Separate from your real name, a pseudonym is a search-resistant name that can't be easily linked to your home address, ID documentation, employer, and other personal information. While separate from your real name, pseudonyms are still persistent in nature, meaning that you can accumulate reputation and relationships over time using it. Reddit users posting content under assumed names are an example of pseudonyms that shield identities but generate reputation and relationships over time.

Sample Sentences
Part of the attraction of building a life in a digital world like Second Life is the opportunity to construct a new identity around a **pseudonym** and a customized avatar.

Nicolas Cage, born Nicholas Coppola, used a **pseudonym** rather than his real family name in order to forge his own independent career path.

Most users on the app prefer to use a **pseudonym** rather than to reveal their real name to strangers.

Quotes
I chose a pseudonym, Chris Marker, pronounceable in most languages, because I was very intent on traveling. *Chris Marker*

I chose to publish the first 'Shopaholic' book under
a pseudonym because I wanted it to be judged on its own merits.
Sophie Kinsella

Question
What pseudonyms have you used in the past to conceal your identity?

Remiss

Type: Adjective

Remiss is often used to express failing one's duty or a lack of care and attention to something. The word is often used to discuss the prevention of future actions and paired with "it would be" in a sentence, as shown in the following samples.

Sample Sentences
It would be **remiss** of me not to mention my mom's help in preparing for the wedding.

It would be **remiss** of me not to address how far we've come despite these current difficulties.

Moscow would be **remiss** to ignore calls to participate in the event.

Quotes
I would be remiss if I left the impression that my life has been totally preoccupied with scholarly research. *Douglass North*

I have a lot of hobbies and I can be very remiss in reminding myself to go down to the basement to work. *Geddy Lee*

Question
Have you been remiss of contacting your family recently or remiss of spending more time with friends?

Risk-reward analysis

Type: Noun

Risk-reward analysis is a decision-making process that involves assessing the potential benefits (rewards or gains) against the potential downsides (risks or losses) of a particular action, investment, project, or decision. This type of analysis is used in various fields, including finance, business, and project management, to evaluate whether the potential benefits of a course of action outweigh the potential risks.

Sample Sentences

After conducting our **risk-reward analysis**, we came to the conclusion that now wasn't the right time to invest in a second apartment.

I will think about this opportunity, but first, I need to do some basic **risk-reward analysis** before making a decision.

Before accepting the job offer, Sarah wanted to do a proper **risk-reward analysis** to ensure that the higher salary was worth the longer commute and increased workload.

Question

Is there a space in your life where risk-reward analysis could be applied where it is currently not?

Sanguine

Type: Adjective

Originating from the Latin term *sanguis,* meaning *blood*, sanguine was originally meant to describe someone's red complexion as a sign of an optimistic outlook. Today, sanguine is an adjective for someone who is cheerfully confident. For instance, if you're sanguine about a situation, that means you are optimistic that everything's going to work out fine.

Sample Sentences

Economic commentators are broadly **sanguine** about the short-term economic situation.

It's difficult to be **sanguine** about the political and economic horizon during this period of division and unrest.

I was strangely **sanguine** about my prospects walking into my nineteenth job interview.

Quotes

That glorious vision of doing good is so often the sanguine mirage of so many good minds. *Charles Dickens*

He was trying to gather up the scarlet threads of life and weave them into a pattern; to find his way through the sanguine labyrinth of passion through which he was wandering. *Oscar Wilde*

I feel sanguine enough to say that there has never been a better set of conditions for open democratic politics because there is no need for unified front politics. *Lee Kuan Yew*

Question

How do you maintain a sanguine outlook during challenging times?

Sentient

Type: Adjective

Sentient is an adjective that means to be alive and consciously feel or sense things. Living things such as humans and animals are sentient as they are able to see, smell, communicate, touch, hear, and so on, whereas rocks and sand are considered non-sentient. Other living things, such as plants and even cities, may or may not be sentient depending on who you talk to. Sentient comes from the Latin word *sentient,* which means *feeling.*

Sample Sentences

Sentient robots might one day replace me in human resources, but for the time being, I feel safe in my current job position.

Many vegans espouse a noble belief that humans aren't more important or of a higher order than other **sentient** beings.

New York is a **sentient** city; always recreating itself and responding to inside and outside forces.

Quotes

All sentient beings have the seed of the Buddha within them. *Dalai Lama*

Just being sentient and in a body with the sun coming up is a state of rapture. *Coleman Barks*

Question

What are some of the key characteristics or requirements for something to be sentient?

Spurious

Type: Adjective

Technically speaking, spurious means to be born out of wedlock as an illegitimate birth. However, in general communication, we typically use the word to describe something that is meant to deceive or that is outwardly similar to something but without having its genuine qualities. Examples of things that can't be trusted at face value include spurious ideas, spurious statements, or spurious data patterns, which are false or invalid while masquerading as the truth.

Sample Sentences
Any claims that I was biased in my decision are **spurious** and unfounded.

The aim of the mathematical prediction model is to ignore any **spurious** relationships and hone in on the patterns that matter.

Politicians often accuse each other of constructing **spurious** claims intended to deceive voters.

Quotes
I enjoy reading blogs, but am not interested in having my spurious thoughts out there. *Brian Greene*

Sentimentality, the ostentatious parading of excessive and spurious emotion, is the mark of dishonesty. *James A. Baldwin*

Question
Have you ever been led down the garden path (deceived) by spurious claims from an employer or a salesperson?

Straitlaced

Type: Adjective

Straitlaced means someone who is excessively strict in manners, morals, or opinion. The word is likely to be used disapprovingly, such as describing someone who is overly strict or evasive to challenging expected boundaries of behavior. In other cases, straitlaced might reflect a moderate or even positive assessment of someone, such as a straitlaced role model or a straitlaced employee you can rely on.

Sample Sentences

She is the sort of **straitlaced** employee that fits in well at a consulting company.

No one likes a **straitlaced** overachiever as an elder sibling.

Kim is extremely prim and proper; someone you could describe as **straitlaced**.

Quotes

I guess us folks in California are kind of straitlaced and old-fashioned. *J.R. Rain*

My life won't be a series of either/ors - musician or actor, rock or country, straitlaced or rebellious, this or that, yes or no. *Miley Cyrus*

Question

Which classmate do you remember as a straitlaced student?

Symbiotic

Type: Adjective

Symbiotic describes two or more organisms living together or in close physical proximity. Used more widely, symbiotic refers to a relationship where both parties benefit or rely on each other for support.

Sample Sentences

The partnership between the tech company and the startup was **symbiotic**, as the larger company inherited innovative ideas while the startup received valuable resources.

In a healthy ecosystem, certain plants and fungi have a **symbiotic** relationship, benefiting each other through nutrient exchange.

We have a **symbiotic** relationship where he helps me with learning Japanese and I help him with practicing English.

Quotes

Dogs and humans are symbiotic species. We need each other. *Cynthia Heimel*

I don't think anywhere is there a symbiotic relationship between caddie and player like there is in golf. *Johnny Miller*

The cows shorten the grass, and the chickens eat the fly larvae and sanitize the pastures. This is a symbiotic relation. *Joel Salatin*

Question

What are two things in your life that possess a symbiotic relationship, in that they rely on each other and become stronger in unison?

Tacit

Type: Adjective

Something that is expressed, implied, or indicated without words (unspoken) can be called tacit. Lawyers, for example, talk about tacit agreements where parties give their silent consent and raise no objections. The word tacit comes from Middle French and Latin meaning *silent*.

Sample Sentences
The athlete kept his **tacit** knowledge at a distance from the investigators.

By not attending the meeting, you will be providing your **tacit** approval for others to also not attend.

Silence may be taken to mean **tacit** agreement.

Quotes
Revolutionary constituencies always involve a tacit alliance between the least alienated and the most oppressed. *David Graeber*

The rules of friendship are tacit, unconscious; they are not rational. In business, though, you have to think rationally. *Steven Pinker*

Question
Do you have any tacit agreements with a friend or a colleague about how you should cooperate or work together?

Tactile

Type: Adjective

Tactile is something that is perceptible by the sense of touch, such as a physical book written in braille or eating with your hands. Tactile can also describe a sensory experience such as retail shopping.

Sample Sentences

There is a huge **tactile** difference between living in the tropical north of the country and the mild weather of the south.

Like humans, pets have a **tactile** preference for sleeping on soft surfaces like the bed or the couch.

Apple's flagship stores are designed to give customers a **tactile** experience.

Quotes

I'm very tactile. I'm a big hugger, one of those huggy people. *Kathryn Hahn*

There's something very satisfying about creating a tactile product. *Chad Hurley*

Writing has always had a tactile quality for me. It's a physical experience. *Paul Auster*

Question

Do you have a memorable in-person retail experience? I.E., an in-person purchase of a watch, a suit, clothes, an iPhone, a new car, etc. What tactile stimuli formed part of this pleasurable experience?

Tchotchke

Type: Noun

Derived from Yiddish, a tchotchke is a trinket, knick-knack, or another small and cheap object—usually plastic—that is decorative rather than strictly functional. Examples of tchotchkes include decorative figures, work-related memorabilia, and Christmas trinkets.

Sample Sentences

After converting to minimalism and living a more intentional way of life, I decided to remove the many worthless **tchotchkes** clogging my shelves and desk space.

While it's no more than a cheap **tchotchke**, this gift from my Grandma holds sentimental value to me and is a reminder of our time together.

China's south-eastern city of Yiwu is sometimes described as "the city the dollar store built" because of all the plastic **tchotchkes** manufactured there.

Quotes

I'm not a big fan of the tchotchkes. It always reminds me of a Grandma's stuffy home with a million Santa dolls. *Jeremiah Brent*

Question

Are there any tchotchkes that adorn your office or home?

Timeless

Type: Adjective

Timeless is something that is just as good or relevant now as when it was created and therefore unchanged or unaffected by time. Timeless is similar to the word *classic*, and both words carry a positive association and bode well as a compliment, i.e., a timeless design, work, or piece of literature.

Sample Sentences
The novel's themes of love and loss are so deeply human that they remain **timeless**, resonating with readers across eras.

It felt like a **timeless** state of bliss.

A **timeless** design is the pinnacle achievement for any artist.

Quotes
I want to make timeless movies. *Fred Durst*

The word of God gives us timeless hope. *Lailah Gifty Akita*

You get a timeless cool card in New York. *Vin Diesel*

Question
What comes to mind when you think of a timeless city?

Transient

Type: Adjective or noun

Transient is to pass quickly in and out of existence. It's often used as an adjective to describe something that is fleeting or temporary, such as passing through a place with only a brief stay. You might also use this word to describe something that always changes or moves around such as someone who is constantly moving from city to city.

Sample Sentences
I enjoyed a **transient** and rugged lifestyle of travel and discovery in my youth. (adjective)

While being very popular, the current level of attention is **transient** at best. (adjective)

My days of living as a poor musician and **transient** are coming to an end; I want to optimize my opportunities for stability and growth going forward. (noun)

Quotes
Beauty is transient and changes with time. *Aishwarya Rai Bachchan*

Methods are transient: personality is enduring. *Edward Hopper*

Hollywood is full of transients. Everybody comes from somewhere else. *Poppy Montgomery*

Question
Is there someone in your life who you could describe as transient because they move from city to city or from one job to another?

Utility

Type: Noun

Related to the verb *utilize*, utility is a noun meaning something useful or designed for use, which is another way of saying *use* (noun form). Utility can also be used as a noun to describe public services (i.e., electricity, gas, water).

Utility can be paired with *marginal* (marginal utility) to describe the additional satisfaction or benefit (utility) that a consumer derives from buying an additional unit of a commodity or service. Other uses of the word include *utility knife* (a type of general-purpose knife) and *utility belt* (a type of belt with multiple pouches and loops providing easy access to various tools).

Sample Sentences

This product might look beautiful but there's a total absence of **utility**.

What **utility** does a swimming pool have in the dead of winter?

I wonder about the **utility** of riding my bicycle to work to reduce pollution when so many people drive cars.

The concept of marginal **utility** helps economists understand how individuals make decisions by evaluating the additional satisfaction gained from consuming one more unit of a product.

Quotes

Money has no utility to me beyond a certain point. *Bill Gates*

There's a utility in the democracy refreshing itself on an ongoing basis. *Barack Obama*

Question

What new utility has the Internet provided you during the pandemic?

Vigilant

Type: Adjective

To be vigilant is to be alert and watchful in avoiding danger. The word is derived from Latin to keep watch and to stay awake. For added emphasis, vigilant can also be combined with *hyper*.

Sample Sentences

I am hyper**vigilant** to avoid the same fate as my parents.

Be **vigilant** about others listening to what we say.

When taking the subway, be **vigilant** of your wallet.

Quotes

Be vigilant; guard your mind against negative thoughts. *Gautama Buddha*

I like the privacy of my life and I protect it quite vigilantly. *Nicole Kidman*

Though we are optimistic, we must remain vigilant and maintain a sense of urgency. *Jeff Bezos*

Question

What can you do to be more vigilant regarding your health?

Vigilante

Type: Noun

A vigilante is someone who takes the law into their own hands through unofficial channels, such as trying to catch or punish someone directly and taking the law into their own hands. While a vigilante might be a self-appointed doer of justice, they are probably not acting within the legal confines. Vigilante derives from the previous word *vigilant,* which means to keep a watchful or close eye on something or someone.

Sample Sentences
There's no need to take the law into your hands and behave like a rogue **vigilante**.

There is unsaid support for the **vigilantes** among government officials.

Armed **vigilantes** are expected to confront the protesters at the next rally.

Quotes
Don't underestimate the power of the vigilante consumer. *Anita Roddick*

Punitive murder by the police and by vigilantes has existed in all societies at some point, and probably still exists in most. *Teju Cole*

Question
Have you had any close contact with vigilantes? If not, what films can you think of that feature a character who fits the definition of a vigilante?

Visceral

Type: Adjective

Visceral means something which is felt intuitively or deep down as a gut feeling. The word comes from *viscera*, which are the internal organs of the body—including the heart, liver, and intestines. A visceral feeling may not have a rational explanation, such as an unexplained phobia or an inexplicable feeling of knowing the right option.

Sample Sentences
His words only added a **visceral** punch to my already broken heart.

The documentary provoked a **visceral** reaction in me.

I could not explain it, but I had a **visceral** sense of unease about moving there.

Quotes
I've always been very visceral in that I feel things very deeply. *P.J Harvey*

What makes a story is how well it manages to connect with the reader, the visceral effect it has. *Len Wein*

I do feel visceral revulsion at the burka because for me it is a symbol of the oppression of women. *Richard Dawkins*

Question
Have you recently had a visceral reaction to something? How did it feel?

Volition

Type: Noun

Volition means the act of making a decision or the power to choose and is derived from the Latin verb *belle*, which means *to will* or *to wish*. This word is useful for emphasizing that a decision was made consciously or deliberately and is often paired with the word "own" or a pronoun. Volition is another way of saying "by choice".

Sample Sentences
He left the company of his own **volition**.

The decision to switch classes was made against her **volition**.

I made this decision by my own **volution**.

Quotes
I joined the local athletics club when I was 12, that's what I did. I did it of my own volition. *Sebastian Coe*

To me, songs come of their own volition - and with an open-ended philosophy. *Rufus Wainwright*

Question
Do you make decisions of your own volition? Or are you often pressed by someone else into making important choices?

Voracious

Type: Adjective

Voracious is an adjective used to describe a strong craving and comes from the Latin *vorāre*, meaning *to devour*. Voracious is usually associated with having a wolflike appetite for something, such as eating, drinking, reading, writing, or even being a voracious lover. The word may carry some connotation of being greedy or overzealous, but generally speaking, is not negative.

Sample Sentences
I am a **voracious** user of this app.

Reading non-fiction is a strong sign of being a **voracious** learner.

I have a **voracious** appetite when it comes to pizza.

Quotes
I have a voracious appetite for all things, worldly and unworldly. *Jimmy Page*

Develop into a lifelong self-learner through voracious reading; cultivate curiosity and strive to become a little wiser every day. *Charlie Munger*

Question
Aside from reading, where else might you use the word voracious to describe an insatiable thirst to devour?

Thank you.

We hope you found value in this guide to improve your vocabulary. If you enjoyed this book, you might to consider reading the next book in this series: The English Vocabulary Builder Vol. 2, which is packed with more hand-selected vocabulary to expand your surface lexicon.

For feedback or suggestions, please contact us at lingovalley@gmail.com.

SEARCH "LINGO VALLEY"
ON AMAZON
TO FIND IT EASILY (AS
WELL AS OTHER BOOKS)

Made in the USA
Las Vegas, NV
03 February 2024

85257914R00062